FARM ANIMALS

PIGS

by Sheri Doyle

Consulting Editor: Gail Saunders-Smith, PhD

Consultant: Dr. Celina Johnson, College of Agriculture
California State University, Chico

CAPSTONE PRESS
a capstone imprint

Pebble Plus is published by Capstone Press,
1710 Roe Crest Drive, North Mankato, Minnesota 56003.
www.capstonepub.com

Library of Congress Cataloging-in-Publication Data
Doyle, Sheri.
Pigs / by Sheri Doyle.
p. cm.—(Pebble plus. Farm animals)
Includes bibliographical references and index.
Summary: "Simple text and full-color photographs provide a brief introduction to pigs"—Provided by publisher.
ISBN 978-1-4296-8647-1 (library binding)
ISBN 978-1-62065-303-6 (ebook PDF)
1. Swine—Juvenile literature. I. Title.
SF395.5.D69 2013
636.4—dc23

2011049980

Editorial Credits
Erika L. Shores, editor; Ashlee Suker, designer; Marcie Spence, media researcher; Eric Manske, production specialist

Photo Credits
Corbis: Russ Munn/AgStock Images, 11; Dreamstime: Mantonino, 9, Martinedegraaf, 17; fotolia: Lyrk, 7;
iStockphoto: BertBeekmans, 13, Rhoberazzi, 19; Shutterstock: Galyna Andrushko, 5, jokter, cover, 1,
Lynne Carpenter, 21, Vphoto, 15

Note to Parents and Teachers

The Farm Animals series supports national science standards related to life science. This book
describes and illustrates pigs. The images support early readers in understanding the text. The
repetition of words and phrases helps early readers learn new words. This book also introduces
early readers to subject-specific vocabulary words, which are defined in the Glossary section.
Early readers may need assistance to read some words and to use the Table of Contents,
Glossary, Read More, Internet Sites, and Index sections of the book.

Printed in the United States of America in North Mankato, Minnesota.
012014   007940R

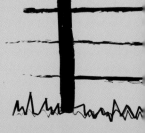

Table of Contents

Meet the Pigs

The morning sun shines

on the farmyard.

Oink! Here come some pigs!

They sniff the ground

with their snouts.

Pigs have thick bodies covered with hair. Some pigs have ears that stick up. Others have floppy ears. Pigs walk on sturdy hooves.

On the Farm

Pigs eat feed made from corn,

soybeans, and other food.

Some pigs graze

in fenced pastures.

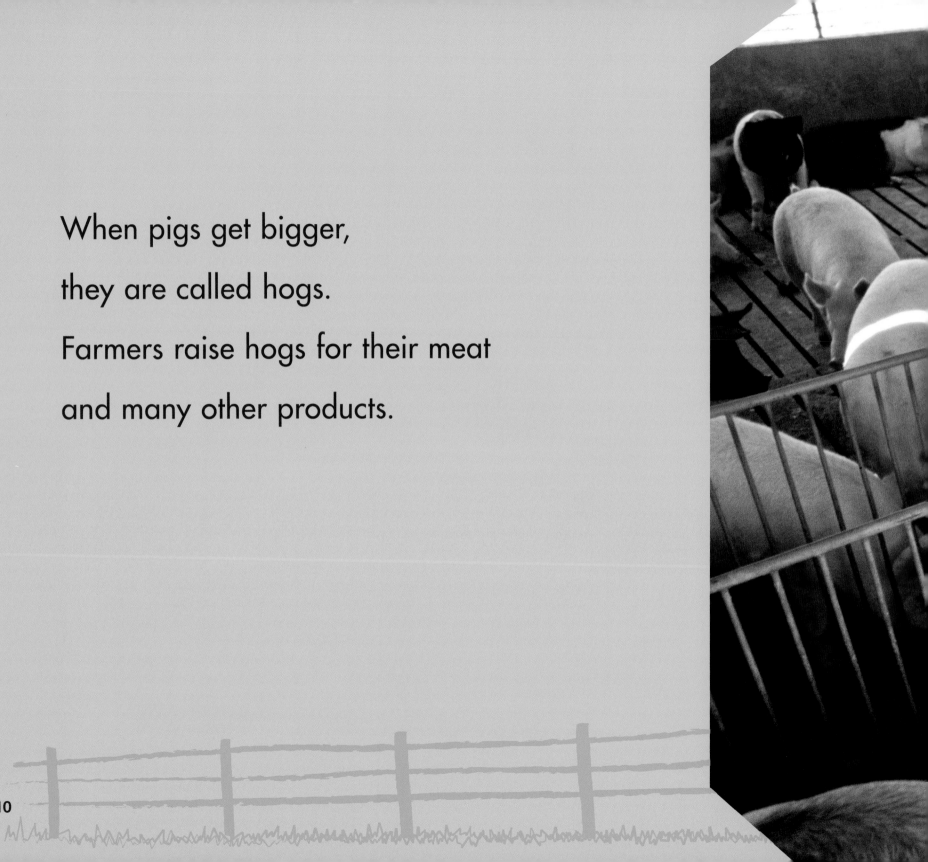

When pigs get bigger,
they are called hogs.
Farmers raise hogs for their meat
and many other products.

Some hogs grow to be

1,000 pounds (454 kilograms)

or more. That's as heavy as

a grand piano!

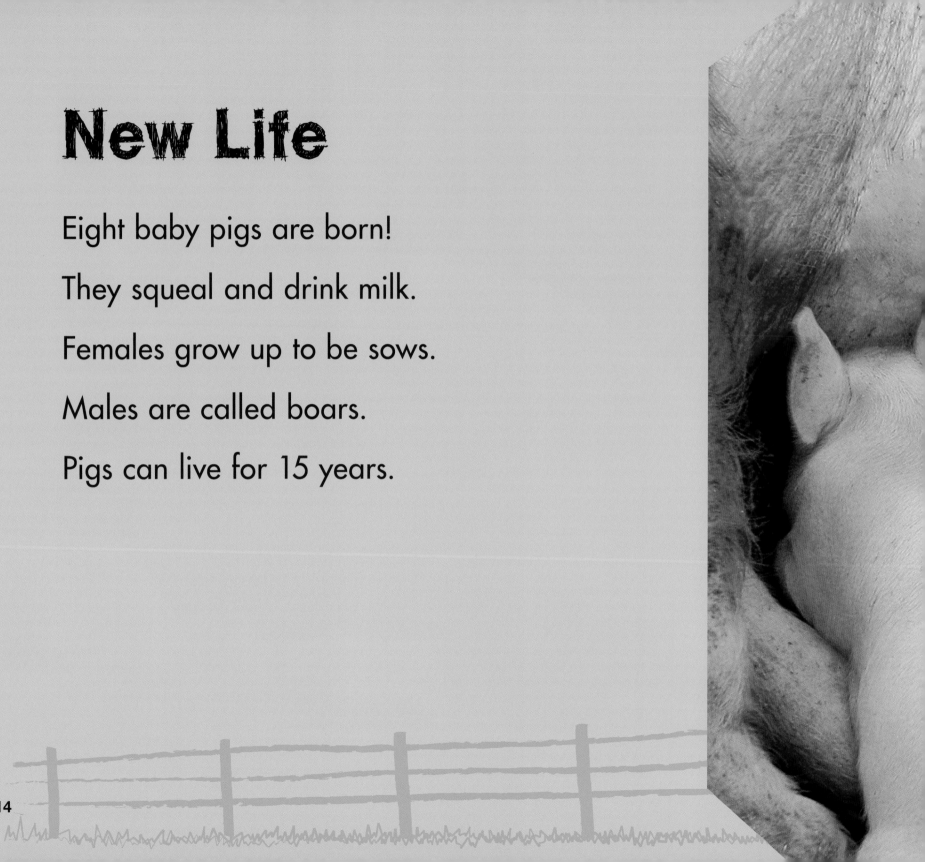

New Life

Eight baby pigs are born!

They squeal and drink milk.

Females grow up to be sows.

Males are called boars.

Pigs can live for 15 years.

Playtime

Pigs are smart and playful.

Some farmers give pigs balls

to play with.

Happy pigs grunt.

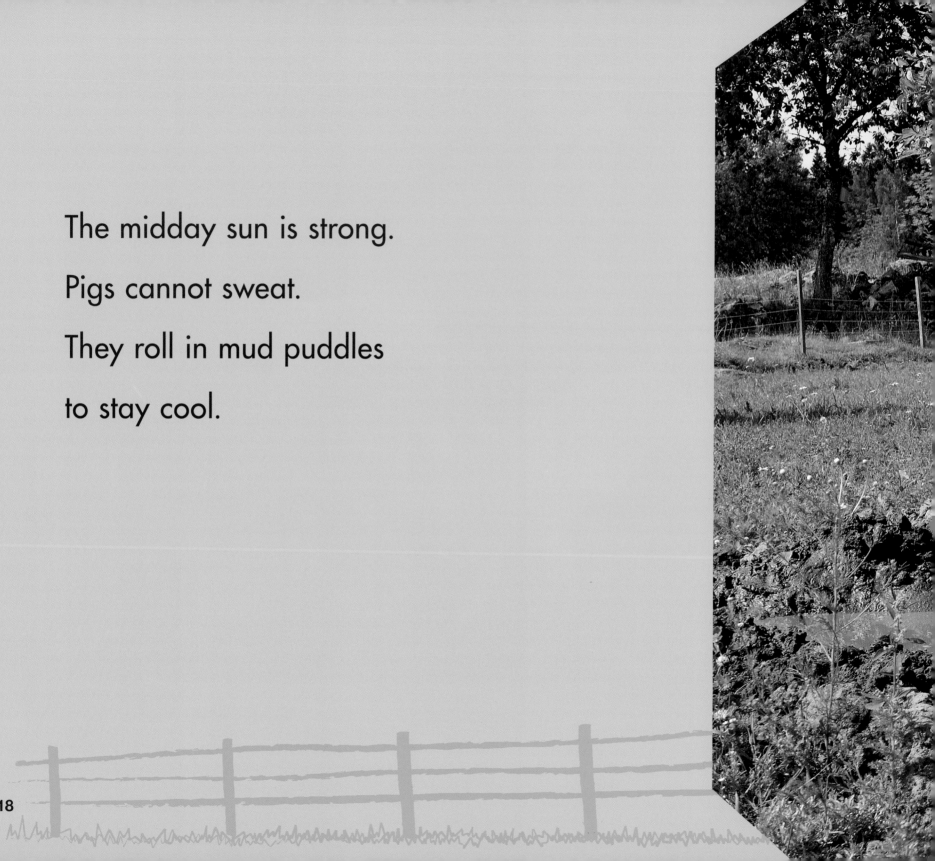

The midday sun is strong.

Pigs cannot sweat.

They roll in mud puddles

to stay cool.

Time to Rest

Pigs sleep in barns.

They snuggle on floors

padded with straw.

Glossary

boar—an adult male pig

feed—food that comes in the form of mash or pellets

graze—to eat grass

hog—a pig that weighs more than 120 pounds (54 kilograms)

hoof—a pig's foot; more than one hoof is hooves

pasture—a grassy area that pigs and other animals feed upon

snout—a pig's nose

sow—an adult female pig

Read More

Dolphin, Colleen. *Playful Pigs.* Farm Pets. Edina, Minn.: ABDO Pub., 2010.

Kalman, Bobbie. *Baby Pigs.* It's Fun to Learn about Baby Animals. New York: Crabtree., 2010.

Macken, JoAnn Early. *Pigs.* Animals that Live on the Farm. Pleasantville, N.Y.: Weekly Reader Pub., 2010.

Internet Sites

FactHound offers a safe, fun way to find Internet sites related to this book. All of the sites on FactHound have been researched by our staff.

Here's all you do:

Visit *www.facthound.com*

Type in this code: 9781429686471

Check out projects, games and lots more at
www.capstonekids.com

Index

Word Count: 163
Grade: 1
Early-Intervention Level: 14